MUSICAL INSTRUMENTS

Meryl Doney

Gareth Stevens Publishing
A WORLD ALMANAC EDUCATION GROUP COMPANY

About this Book

All over the world, music brings people together. Since ancient times, musicians everywhere have used local materials and methods to make their own instruments. This book looks at many different kinds of instruments. Each left-hand page describes a type of instrument and includes a map to show where it comes from. Full-color photographs show some of the rich variety of musical instruments in the world. Each right-hand page provides step-by-step instructions and illustrations for making one of the instruments shown. You can add decorations and modifications of your own. Besides being decorative, musical instruments have to work. You need patience and perseverance both to make them and to play them well. When you have made some instruments and have become good at playing them, you can form an orchestra or band (see page 29).

Most of the steps for making the projects in this book are easy to follow, but wherever you see this symbol, ask for help from an adult.

Measurement Conversions:
1 inch = 25.4 millimeters (mm)
1 inch = 2.54 centimeters (cm)

Please visit our web site at: www.garethstevens.com
For a free color catalog describing Gareth Stevens Publishing's list of high-quality books and multimedia programs, call 1-800-542-2595 (USA) or 1-800-387-3178 (Canada). Gareth Stevens Publishing's fax: (414) 332-3567.

Library of Congress Cataloging-in-Publication Data

Doney, Meryl, 1942-
      Musical instruments / by Meryl Doney.
          p. cm. — (Crafts from many cultures)
      Includes bibliographical references and index.
      Contents: A musical history — Sticks and stones — Australia, Zimbabwe, and Mexico — Shake and rattle — Southern Africa and Togo — Bells on their toes — India and Zimbabwe — Hanging sounds — Mexico and Indonesia — "Tongues" and thumbs — Pakistan and Kenya — Flutes and whistles — Central America, Mozambique, and Peru — Types of pipes — Bolivia, Nigeria, and Syria — Strings and bows — Mozambique and Jordan — Guitars old and new — China and Zimbabwe — Frame drums — North America — Great drums — Kenya, Gambia, Zimbabwe, and Tunisia — Making music.
      ISBN 0-8368-4045-3 (lib. bdg.)
      1. Musical Instruments—Construction—Juvenile literature. [1. Musical Instruments—Construction. 2. Musical Instruments.] I. Title.
ML460.D58 2004
784.192'3—dc22   2003055859

This North American edition first published in 2004 by
Gareth Stevens Publishing
A World Almanac Education Group Company
330 West Olive Street, Suite 100
Milwaukee, Wisconsin 53212 USA

This U.S. edition copyright © 2004 by Gareth Stevens, Inc. Original edition copyright © 1995 by Franklin Watts. Text © 1995 by Meryl Doney.

First published as *World Crafts: Musical Instruments* in 1995 by Franklin Watts, 96 Leonard Street, London WC2A 4XD, England. Additional end matter copyright © 2004 by Gareth Stevens, Inc.

Franklin Watts series editor: Annabel Martin
Franklin Watts editor: Jane Walker
Design: Visual Image
Artwork: Ruth Levy
Photography: Peter Millard

Additional photographs:
Christine Osborne Pictures: 12 (bottom);
Robert Harding Picture Library: 14 (top), 22 (right), 24 (right).

Gareth Stevens editor: JoAnn Early Macken
Gareth Stevens cover design: Kami Koenig

Printed in the United States of America

1 2 3 4 5 6 7 8 9 08 07 06 05 04

Contents

A Musical History

Making music is as old as the human race. No one can tell exactly when musical instruments were first used. People probably used themselves as instruments right from the beginning. They clapped their hands, stamped their feet, and, of course, used their voices. People in ancient times used natural objects such as wood, stone, and bone to make different sounds. Simple rhythm instruments existed in Europe twenty-five thousand years ago! Long ago, people used wind instruments such as flutes and horns in religious ceremonies and as a means to signal to one another. As civilizations developed in Europe and the Middle East, more sophisticated instruments were made. They began to be used for entertainment as well.

Music is made in every culture. It is used for religious worship, family and state occasions, parties, and entertainment. Although musical styles differ from time to time and from one culture to another, the kinds of instruments that people make are remarkably similar worldwide. Drums, flutes, horns, rattles, and stringed instruments appear almost everywhere in the world.

Instruments can be made simply from local materials or by using complicated computer technology. All it takes to play some instruments well is a good sense of timing and rhythm. Others need years of practice. In either case, people get great pleasure from playing and listening to music.

Your Own Music-Making Kit

Many of the instruments in this book are made from natural materials. Others use manufactured items such as cardboard tubes, tin cans, and bottle caps. Put together your own music-making kit by collecting materials you may need. Keep small items in plastic jars and the rest in a big cardboard box with a set of tools.

Here are some of the most useful items for your music-making kit:

hammer • back saw • hacksaw • vise • awl • pliers • hand drill • wood file or rasp • scissors • heavy craft knife • metal ruler • brushes • white acrylic paint • poster paints • varnish • PVA (wood) glue • strong glue • plastic modeling material • modeling clay • wire

• wood • dowel • leather • bamboo • string • masking tape • paper • pen • pencil • felt-tipped pens • needle and thread • metal skewer • nails • wooden block to hammer on • sandpaper • newspaper to work on • protective gloves • apron • paper towels

Ideas for decoration

When you make a musical instrument, you can invent your own style of decoration. Try using different colors, patterns, and shapes. If the instruments come from a culture different than your own and you need some inspiration, visit your local or school library. Look for books about the countries and the people that interest you.

See if you can find the different ways in which they decorate the instruments they make.

Trace patterns and shapes or adapt them freely for your own use. We have used this method for the prayer drum on page 25. The design was taken from one sewn in beads on the back of a North American Indian baby carrier called a cradleboard.

Sticks and Stones

Rhythm is essential to making music, and clapping is one of the simplest ways to keep a beat. Some of the first musical instruments people invented were designed to do their clapping for them. In ancient Egypt, ivory clappers were made for just that purpose.

We still use this method to beat out a rhythm. The modern wooden clappers shown below left are made by the Aboriginal people of Australia. They are carved from hardwood, and a hot metal skewer is used to burn in the decorations.

Shakers or rattles can be made from animal or sea shells, hide and leather, horn, wood, and metal. Leg rattles like the one on the right are called *amahlwayi*. They are made from insect cocoons by the Ndebele tribe of Zimbabwe. The Mexican scraper (top left), which is called a *guiro*, is sounded by running a stick along the ridges cut into the wood.

Instruments that make use of the sounds made by natural objects such as stone, wood, or metal are called ideophones. They can be played by stamping with the feet, shaking, rattling, hitting with another object, banging or scraping together, or plucking.

Make Your Own Rhythm Sticks

You will need: dowel, at least 16 inches long ▪ vise ▪ saw ▪ sandpaper ▪ wood file or rasp ▪ protective gloves ▪ metal meat skewer ▪ pliers ▪ poster paints ▪ varnish

Can you think of other ideas for sound makers? Gently tap as many things as you can find with a dowel beater. Be careful not to try anything fragile! Most materials have a natural note when they are sounded. Here are some suggestions: milk cartons (the note can be altered by pouring in some water), saucepan lids, radiators, waste baskets, tiles, a nail hung on a thread, wooden floorboards, and tin trays.

1 Grip the dowel in the vise and saw off two 8-inch lengths.

2 Smooth the ends with sandpaper or shape them to a point with a file or rasp.

3 To decorate sticks Aboriginal style, put on protective gloves. Grip the skewer with the pliers and hold it in a gas flame until it is very hot. Lay the hot skewer across the wood in the vise so that it burns a brown mark. The end of the skewer makes a round dot.

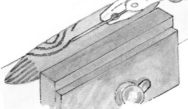

Repeat, making more marks, to form a pattern. When you are finished, run cold water over the skewer to cool it.

4 You can also decorate your sticks by painting and varnishing them.

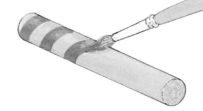

You can make a guiro scraper by wrapping and tying string around a large plastic bottle. Then scrape it with a stick.

Shake and Rattle

When a gourd or a seed pod dries in the sun, the flesh shrivels up, leaving the hard seeds to rattle around inside. These natural rattles have long been used in music and magical rituals. The black gourd rattle from Southern Africa (bottom right) is a good example.

A gourd is also the basis for the *kass-kassa* (sometimes called a *shekere* or *kabassa*). This one (top right) was made by Issifou Amadou in Togo. The calabash gourds are specially grown and trained to the correct shape. The covering is made from elephant grass seeds threaded on a string mesh. The shaker is held in the hand, and the seeds are shaken against the surface or swirled around the gourd.

The hand-made *tioco-tioco-ni* (chiko-chiko-ni), or basketwork shaker (top left), has a gourd or tin base. Seeds rattle against it. The shaker is modeled on the shape of a gourd.

Weave a Basket Shaker

You will need: compass ■ cork tile ■ newspaper ■ craft knife ■ awl ■ 15-inch lengths of cane ■ string or raffia ■ ball ■ dried chickpeas or beans ■ masking tape

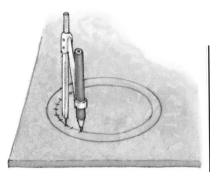

1 Draw two circles, radius 1 $\frac{3}{8}$ and 1 $\frac{3}{4}$ inches, on the cork tile. Set the compass to $\frac{3}{8}$ inch. Divide the inner circle into 23 sections.

2 On newspaper, cut around the outer cork circle with a craft knife. Make a hole at each point on the inner circle with the awl.

3 Soak the cane in water until it is pliable. Push a piece of cane through each hole in the cork about 2 inches. Weave the ends together

4 On the top side, tie the end of the string to the base of a cane. Weave in and out. Push the string down as you go. Use different colors to make stripes. Help your work bend outward by putting a ball inside the canes.

5 After about 2 $\frac{1}{2}$ inches of weaving, remove the ball and begin to draw the weaving inward toward a point. Before closing the top, drop in a handful of dried chickpeas or beans.

6 Divide the ends of the canes into two bunches. Form them into a circular handle. Secure it with masking tape. Bind the handle with string or raffia.

Bells on their Toes

Bells and jingles are examples of metal ideophones. A bell has a loose clapper that hits against the metal sides. Bells are often used by dancers because they emphasize the body's movements. The *ghungaroo* (right) are brass dancing bells from India. They can be worn around the ankle, wrist, or waist on a string or belt. Morris dancers in the United Kingdom use similar bells for their dances.

Metal jingles, which are similar to bells, have a long history in dance and as an aid to prayer and worship. The *sistrum*, which is a metal and wire shaker, can be traced back to ancient Egypt and Roman Pompeii. It is used today by the Coptic church of Ethiopia. The wooden sistrum (bottom) comes from Harare, Zimbabwe. It is made with recycled bottle caps.

The tambourine (top left) is also from Harare. Tambourines, or frame drums, originated in the Middle East.

Cookie-Tin Tambourine

You will need: small, shallow cookie tin ▪ can opener ▪ hammer ▪ wooden block ▪ file ▪ felt-tipped pen ▪ awl ▪ heavy craft knife ▪ bottle caps ▪ pliers ▪ plastic modeling material ▪ coat hanger wire

You can make a sistrum from a branch with its bark removed. Use the same method as for the tambourine shown here. Put the branch in a vise and drill holes for the wire. Decorate it with a hot skewer (see page 7) or paint and varnish it.

1 Remove the base of the tin with a can opener.

Hammer the rough edges flat on the wooden block. Smooth with the file.

2 Mark a rectangle, 1 x 2 inches, on the side of the tin. Add a line down the center of the rectangle. Repeat at 2-inch intervals until you have five rectangles.

3 Punch a hole with the awl halfway down both sides of each rectangle as shown.

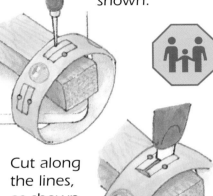

Cut along the lines, as shown, by pressing on the tin with a heavy craft knife.

4 Hold each bottle cap in the pliers. Flatten with the hammer on the wooden block.

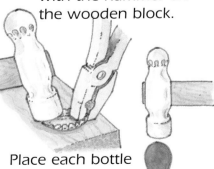

Place each bottle cap on plastic modeling material, and punch a hole in the center with the awl.

5 Cut five 2-inch pieces of wire. On inside of tin, bend back two sides of rectangles to form tabs.

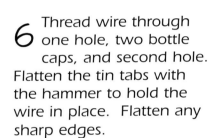

6 Thread wire through one hole, two bottle caps, and second hole. Flatten the tin tabs with the hammer to hold the wire in place. Flatten any sharp edges.

Hanging Sounds

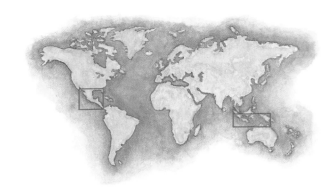

Wind chimes like these from Mexico (left) are another form of ideophone. Natural objects such as wood, stone, or fired clay all have their own particular tones if they are suspended and allowed to vibrate freely. Try this for yourself. Tie a piece of thread around a nail. Hold the nail up so that it does not touch anything else, and then hit it with a dowel. It should make a ringing sound. Different-sized nails make different notes.

This same principle is also used by the family of instruments that includes the xylophone (wooden bars), the lithophone (stone or slate bars), and the metalophone (metal bars). The bars are suspended above tubes or gourds that act as sound boxes.

Highly developed bar ideophones are found in the gamelan orchestras of Java and Bali in Indonesia. These orchestras provide music for shadow puppet plays. Instruments in the gamelan include large gongs, which are suspended in decorated frames, and the gender, or wooden xylophone (right).

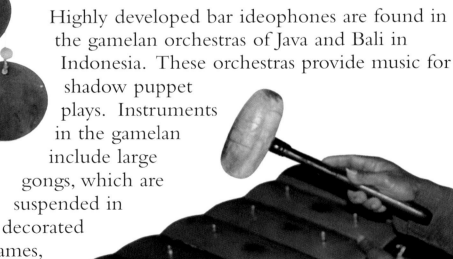

Make Tile Music

If you have access to clay and a kiln, you can make fired-clay bars for your gender. Otherwise, the edging pieces used in tiling work very well.

You will need: cereal box • scissors • 5 toilet paper tubes • strong glue • length of wood, $\frac{1}{2}$ x $\frac{1}{2}$ inch • pencil • twelve $\frac{3}{4}$-inch nails with flat heads • white acrylic paint • poster paints • varnish • 5 tile edging pieces • pliers • 10 small rubber bands

1 Cut the cereal box to the same height as the cardboard tubes. Glue the tubes to the inside of box.

2 Cut two pieces of wood the length of the cereal box. Hold the wood next to the tubes. Mark dots at both ends and between the tubes. Pound a nail into the wood at each dot, leaving $\frac{1}{2}$ inch of each nail sticking up.

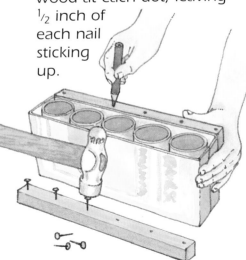

3 Glue the wood along the top edges of the box. Glue two short wood pieces to the base of the box for feet. Paint with white acrylic paint, decorate with poster paints, and varnish.

4 Keep one piece of tile at full length. Shorten the next tile by gently breaking about $\frac{1}{2}$ inch off one end with the pliers. Shorten the next tile by 1 inch and so on until the fifth tile is 2 inches shorter. (Be sure to wrap and throw away the sharp pieces of tile.)

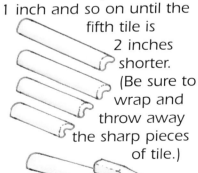

5 Stretch rubber bands from nail to nail along the wood on both sides of the box. Suspend the tiles by twisting the rubber bands and pushing the bars between them along the length of the instrument as shown. Check the note of each tile with a piano. Tune by removing a little more tile.

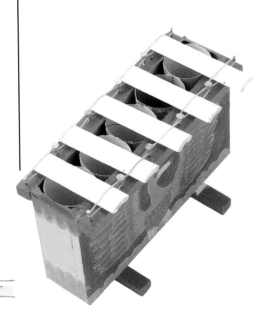

Pakistan and Kenya

"Tongues" and Thumbs

Lingua is the Latin word for tongue. Instruments with a vibrating "tongue" belong to the linguaphone family. Sounds are amplified in a confined space called a sound box or resonator. The Jew's (or jaw) harp works by plucking a "tongue" held between two sides of a frame. The frame is placed between the player's teeth. The player's open mouth is the resonator, and the pitch of the note is changed by moving the tongue or cheeks. This man from Pakistan (right) is playing a jaw harp.

The *mbira*, *sansa*, or "thumb piano" (left) came from Africa. It is held in the palms of the hands. The tongues are held against a bridge on a piece of wood or in a box and plucked with the thumbs. Often, the wood is carved, painted, and decorated. Wire wrapped around the tongues or flattened bottle caps nailed to the box can add extra rattling sounds.

Make a Thumb Piano

You need a length of bamboo cane to make a bamboo jaw harp. Split the cane in half with a craft knife. Make two more cuts, leaving a tongue in between. Hold the harp in your teeth and pluck the tongue to make a note.

You will need: a piece of wooden board, 8 x ½ x 5 inches • ruler • pencil • V-shaped linoleum cutting tool • dark brown shoe polish • polishing cloth • coat hanger wire • wire cutter • pliers • hammer • 10 metal staples

2 Polish wood with dark brown shoe polish. Rub off excess polish.

1 Draw two lines 1 inch and 1 ½ inches from one end of the board. Mark a pattern of lines on the rest of the surface. Carve a pattern into the wood with the linoleum cutting tool. (Always work away from your hands.)

3 Cut seven pieces of coat hanger wire of different lengths from 3 ½ to 5 inches. Hold each one over a very hard surface with the pliers. Flatten one end of each wire with the hammer. Cut two more 4-inch pieces.

4 Lay one piece of 4-inch wire along the second line on the wood and hammer in a staple at each end to hold it in place. Lay all 7 tongues across this wire. Lay the second piece of wire over the tongues along the first line. Staple both ends and between each tongue. Check that tongues make a good, clear sound.

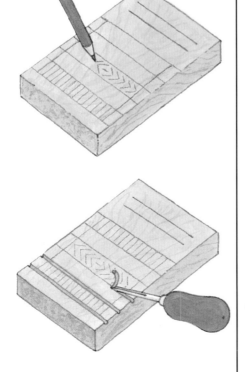

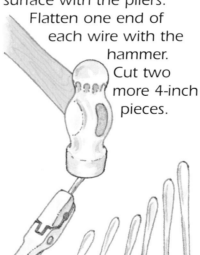

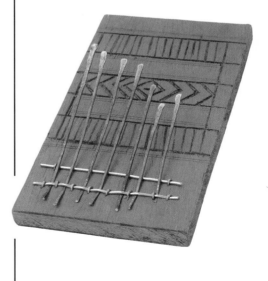

Central America, Mozambique, and Peru

Flutes and Whistles

Long ago, people discovered they could make pleasant sounds by blowing air against a sharp edge. This caused the air to vibrate. Musical instruments that use this principle are called aerophones. They range from simple penny whistles to grand church organs.

Bird bone whistles and flutes date back to the Stone Age. The Andean Indians of South America believed that playing flutes made from the bones of their enemies gave them power over the enemies. The ceramic flute (right) is a copy of one made by the Mayan peoples of Central America some two thousand years ago. It is similar to the recorders played in schools today. The little bird whistle (above) is from Costa Rica.

A sound can also be made by blowing over a hole in a round or shaped vessel. You can change the note by covering and uncovering other holes with your fingers. The round vessel flute (top left) works on this principle. It is made from a dried matamba fruit in Mozambique. The decorated ceramic flute (left), called an *ocarina*, comes from Peru.

16

Make a Clay Flute

You will need: modeling clay ▪ knife ▪ large needle ▪ poster paints ▪ varnish

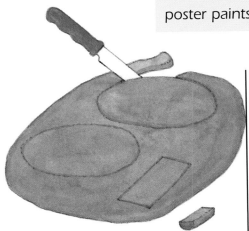

1 Roll a piece of clay flat. Cut out two egg shapes, 3 inches across and 4 inches long, and a rectangle 1 x 2 inches. Make a roll of clay 1 inch long. Cut a thin slice off the side of the roll.

2 Score the edges of each clay piece with the needle and moisten them with water. Form each egg into a bowl shape. Press the two shapes together carefully to form a hollow egg. Score the edges together with the needle, leaving a gap at one end. Smooth the joint with a little water.

3 Form the clay rectangle into a short tube. Attach it to the open end of the egg by scoring. Push the clay roll into the tube, flat side up, leaving a gap to blow through. Smooth the clay with dampened fingers.

4 Use the needle to make four small holes in the upper surface of the egg shape. Make one larger hole on top just behind the blowing hole. Make two small holes in the lower surface.

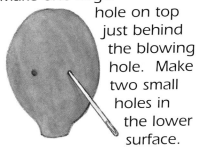

5 Make sure the flute works before it dries hard. Cover the four small holes with your fingers. Gently blow through the end hole.

The sound is made by blown air hitting the far edge of this hole. If the flute does not whistle, adjust the edge of the large hole.

6 Let the flute dry. Paint and varnish it.

Types of Pipes

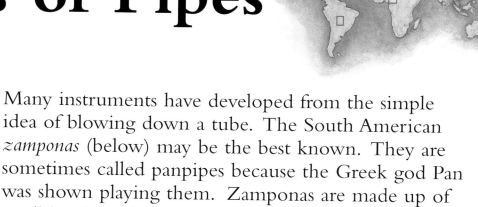

Many instruments have developed from the simple idea of blowing down a tube. The South American *zamponas* (below) may be the best known. They are sometimes called panpipes because the Greek god Pan was shown playing them. Zamponas are made up of small bamboo flutes joined together in a row. They have no finger holes and are closed at one end.

Trumpets and horns are larger versions of the pipe. They are played by vibrating the lips together and using the pipe as the resonator. Horns, as their name suggests, were originally made from animal horns. Trumpets were made from any material that could be hollowed out, such as wood, bamboo, bark, or metal. This decorated gourd horn (left) is from Nigeria.

Another group of pipes uses a thin tongue, called a reed, to vibrate the air. The clarinet, oboe, bassoon, and bagpipes come into this category. The double clarinet (bottom) is from Syria.

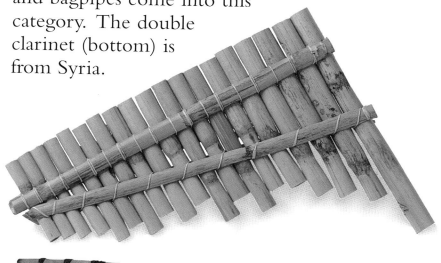

Make a Set of Panpipes

This set of eight pipes will give you a scale of G major. You will need to tune each pipe as you make it, using a piano or recorder (see page 29). If the pipe sounds too low (flat), saw some more off its length. If it is too high (sharp), use it for the next pipe and make a new longer one.

You will need: ½-inch garden bamboo cane, at least 8 sections long • vise • saw • sandpaper • thin stick • ruler • pencil • heavy craft knife • yarn or twine

1 Grip the garden cane in the vise. Divide it into 8 sections by cutting it just below each knot in the bamboo. Remove the pith from inside the tubes with rolled-up sandpaper.

2 Make a mark 4 ¼ inches from one end of the thin stick. Push the stick inside the tube and mark the length. Then hold it next to the tube with the length mark at the end of the tube. Copy the 4 ¼ inch mark to the bamboo. Cut the bamboo to this mark with the saw.

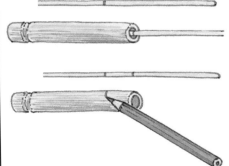

3 Repeat this process with the other 7 pipes, marking them at 3 ¾, 3 ¼, 3, 2 ¾, 2 ½, 2 ¼, and 2 inches. Sand the pipes until they are smooth and check the notes (see above).

4 Cut another piece of bamboo, 5 ½ inches long, with no knots. Split it in half with a heavy craft knife.

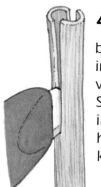

5 Tie a length of yarn around the longest pipe. Lash it diagonally to the half bamboo strip. Wind the yarn around the top and onto the next pipe. Continue until all eight pipes are held firmly in place. Knot the end of the yarn.

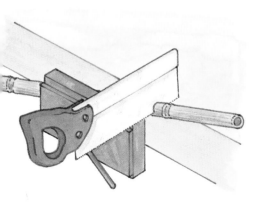

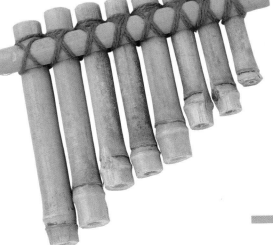

Mozambique and Jordan

Strings and Bows

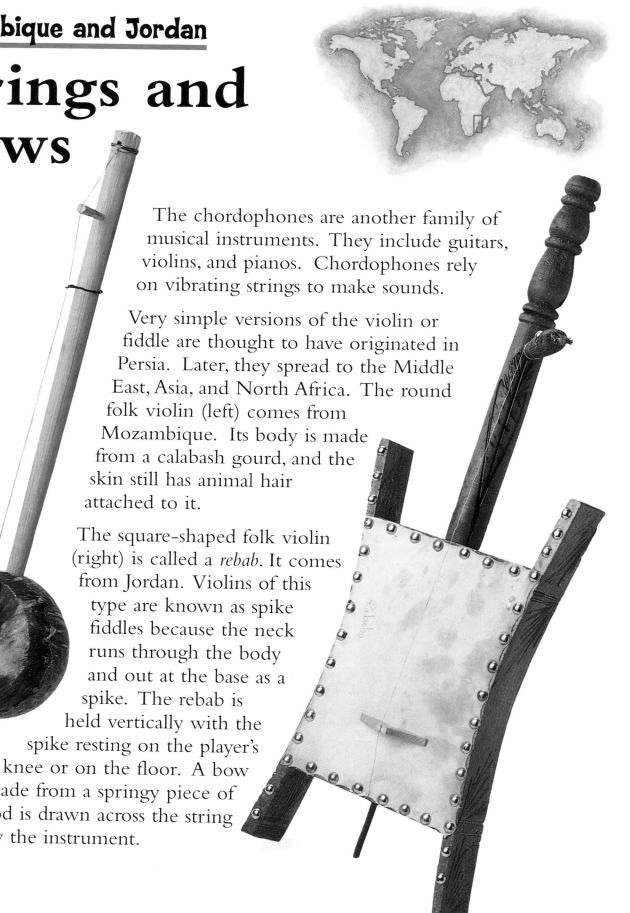

The chordophones are another family of musical instruments. They include guitars, violins, and pianos. Chordophones rely on vibrating strings to make sounds.

Very simple versions of the violin or fiddle are thought to have originated in Persia. Later, they spread to the Middle East, Asia, and North Africa. The round folk violin (left) comes from Mozambique. Its body is made from a calabash gourd, and the skin still has animal hair attached to it.

The square-shaped folk violin (right) is called a *rebab*. It comes from Jordan. Violins of this type are known as spike fiddles because the neck runs through the body and out at the base as a spike. The rebab is held vertically with the spike resting on the player's knee or on the floor. A bow made from a springy piece of wood is drawn across the string to play the instrument.

Make a One-String Violin

This instrument is played by running a bow across the string to vibrate it. (See page 28 for instructions on making a bow.) You can change the note by pressing your finger on the neck end of the string.

You will need: metal skewer ▪ coconut ▪ plastic modeling material ▪ protective gloves ▪ saw ▪ knife ▪ sandpaper ▪ vise ▪ hand drill ▪ ½-inch dowel, 18 inches long ▪ chamois leather ▪ pencil ▪ craft knife ▪ hammer ▪ carpet tacks ▪ stick ▪ guitar string or fuse wire ▪ small bamboo ring

1 Use the skewer to pierce the two coconut "eyes" (flat areas near the point of the nut). Let the milk drain out. Stand the nut on plastic modeling material. Using protective gloves, hold the nut firmly and ask an adult to saw it in half lengthwise.

2 Remove the flesh from one half with a knife. Sand the outside of the shell smooth.

3 Grip the shell in the vise. Drill a row of small holes ½ inch from the edge all around the shell. Drill a ½-inch hole at each end. Drill a small hole ½ inch from the end of the dowel and a larger one 3 inches away.

4 Draw around the nut on the leather. Cut out a shape ¾ inch larger. Soak the leather in water, squeeze it out, and stretch it over the shell to form a drum. Hammer tacks into the small holes, stretching the leather across the nut. Trim off the excess leather and allow it to dry.

5 Push the dowel through the two large holes so that the end sticks out 1 inch. Whittle a peg from the stick and score a groove across the top. Push the peg into the larger hole. Thread the guitar string through the small hole, around the dowel several times, and over the groove in the peg. Pull it tight and tie it around the dowel spike. Add tension to the wire by adding a bridge made from a grooved bamboo ring.

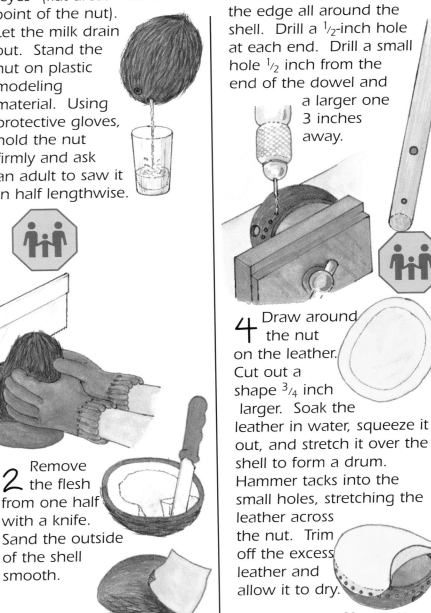

Guitars Old and New

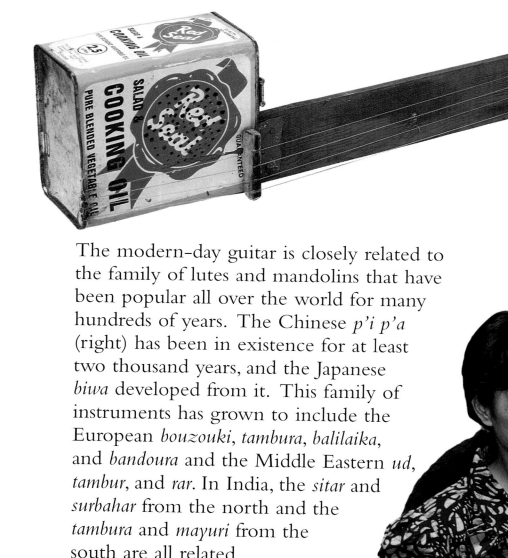

The modern-day guitar is closely related to the family of lutes and mandolins that have been popular all over the world for many hundreds of years. The Chinese *p'i p'a* (right) has been in existence for at least two thousand years, and the Japanese *biwa* developed from it. This family of instruments has grown to include the European *bouzouki*, *tambura*, *balilaika*, and *bandoura* and the Middle Eastern *ud*, *tambur*, and *rar*. In India, the *sitar* and *surbahar* from the north and the *tambura* and *mayuri* from the south are all related.

The *ramkie* is a simple folk guitar from Southern Africa. This one (top) comes from Harare, Zimbabwe. It is made from an old oil can.

Recycle an Oil Can

1 Drain the oil from the can. Punch a number of large holes in the front left side of the can with the awl.

You will need: large, square oil can ▪ awl ▪ hammer ▪ heavy craft knife ▪ detergent ▪ sandpaper ▪ wood file or rasp ▪ two pieces of wood, $\frac{1}{2}$ x 2 $\frac{1}{2}$ x 30 inches and $\frac{1}{2}$ x $\frac{1}{2}$ x 2 $\frac{1}{2}$ inches ▪ wood drill ▪ acrylic paint ▪ stick ▪ nails ▪ four guitar strings ▪ thick rubber strip

2 Cut around three sides of a rectangle on the top right side of the can with a heavy craft knife. Bend the tab upright. Punch four holes through the side and base of the can on the right side. Wash out the can with detergent to remove the rest of the oil. Leave it in a warm place to dry inside.

3 Use sandpaper and a file or rasp to smooth the long wooden fingerboard. Shape and round off the top corners. Drill four holes for pegs. Paint and decorate it as you like.

4 Cut four 2 $\frac{1}{2}$-inch sticks and whittle them into tapering pegs. Cut a deep groove into the top of each peg. Cut four grooves into the top of the 2 $\frac{1}{2}$-inch wooden bridge.

5 Slot the fingerboard into the oil can and nail it in place on the base. Rest it on the edge of a table and nail the tab to the fingerboard.

6 Tie the guitar strings through the holes in the base and wind them around the pegs. Wedge the pegs in the holes and twist them. Slip the wooden bridge under the strings and rest it on the can. Tune the guitar with a piano or recorder.

7 To make a *capo tasto* (to change the key of the strings), cut slits in both ends and the middle of the rubber strip. Thread a 3 $\frac{1}{2}$-inch stick through two slits and lay it across the strings. Wrap the rubber behind the board. Slip the third slit over the end of the stick.

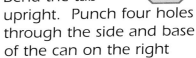
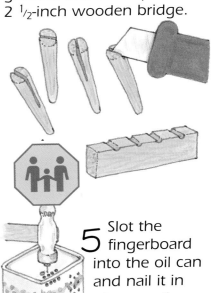

Frame Drums

The word "membrane" means skin. Instruments in the drum family are called membranophones. Drums make sounds by vibrating a skin that is stretched tightly over a frame, which also acts as the resonator. Drums can be cylindrical (open or closed at the end), double headed (with skins at both ends), or bowl shaped. There are many variations to these basic shapes.

The double-sided frame drum (top) is played by rotating the handle. It is also called a prayer drum. Drums like this are often associated with religious ceremonies. The frame drum (right), with its shallow edge and double sides, may have originated in the Middle East. It is also found among the North American Indian and Inuit peoples. The tambourine (see page 11) belongs to this group of drums.

Make a Paper Prayer Drum

This drum is simple to make from stretched paper. It is based on the same principle as the prayer drum shown opposite.

You will need: cardboard tube, about 2 ¹/₂ inches deep and 4 ¹/₂ inches across ▪ layout or copy paper ▪ pencil ▪ scissors ▪ awl ▪ tapered paintbrush handle ▪ ¹/₂-inch dowel, 12 inches long ▪ strong glue ▪ poster paint ▪ PVA glue thinned with water ▪ yarn or string ▪ two small beads ▪ thumbtacks ▪ feathers or streamers

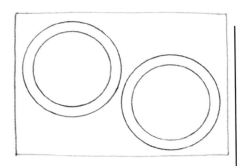

1 Draw around the tube twice on the paper. Cut two circles 1 inch larger than the tube.

2 Use the awl to make a ¹/₂-inch hole in one side of the tube. Enlarge the hole by pushing a paintbrush handle into it. Slot the dowel through the hole and glue it to the opposite side.

3 Draw and paint a design on each paper circle (see page 5). Make scissors cuts all around from the edge to the inside circle. Paint the front and back of both paper disks with the glue mixture.

4 Stretch sticky paper discs over both sides of the tube frame. Glue around the edges. Let it dry.

5 Cut two lengths of yarn about 3 inches long. Tie a bead on one end. Attach a piece of yarn to each side of the drum with thumbtacks. Decorate with feathers or streamers.

Great Drums

Drums play important roles in Africa. Master drummers provide entertainment and accompaniment for dancing. The conical *ntenga* drum (back right) is from Kenya. It is double headed, but only the larger head is played. Ntenga are usually played in pairs of different sizes. The head and stretchers are made from animal skin. A pattern is made by twisting stretchers of different-colored fur.

The large-waisted drum (bottom left), from Gambia, is made from hollowed-out wood and animal skin held by wooden pegs. The smaller African drum (bottom center) is a "footed" type cut from a dried gourd. The double-headed *chigubhu* from Zimbabwe (second from left) is worn around the player's neck, and both ends are played.

Goblet-shaped pottery drums called *darabukke* come from Islamic North Africa. They are often decorated with painting or inlaid work like this one from Tunisia (far right).

Make a Skin Drum

You will need: large cardboard tube ▪ awl ▪ tapered paintbrush handle ▪ two lengths of ½-inch dowel ▪ dark brown wood stain ▪ black felt pen ▪ brown shoe polish ▪ chamois leather ▪ thick cord ▪ needle and yarn

Uncured animal skins are usually used for drum heads because they dry hard and taut. They are difficult to find, and most music shops no longer sell them. However, chamois leather can be bought in car accessory shops and works quite well. Cardboard tubes, plastic piping, wooden barrels, or plant pots make good cylindrical drums. Pottery cooking pots, coconuts, or paint cans are suitable for bowl or vessel drums.

2 Decorate the tube by painting it with dark brown wood stain and black felt pen. Finish with brown shoe polish.

3 Cut a circle of leather 1 inch bigger than the tube. Soak it in water and wring it out. Make four evenly spaced holes in the edge.

4 Place the leather on top of the tube. Run the cord through one hole and under the dowel. Repeat around the other dowels. Wrap the cord around the tube twice. Knot it to keep it secure.

5 With the needle and yarn, sew the edge of the leather to the cord rings, stretching gently all around. Let it dry.

1 Make two holes across from each other in the tube with the awl and a paintbrush handle (see page 25). Push the dowel through both holes so that 1 inch sticks out on each side. Pierce a second pair of holes at right angles to the first. Make these slightly lower down so that the second dowel will push through.

Making Music

Making music together is a worldwide human activity, and children are involved everywhere. They do not usually have formal lessons but are introduced to music making from an early age.

In Africa, mothers rock their babies to sleep, singing nonsense songs that imitate drum rhythms. They carry the babies on their backs to events where music is played.

American Indian children also learn music by copying. They can often reproduce a song perfectly after hearing it only once.

Teenagers are encouraged to go into the wilderness on a "song quest" to find a tune that is uniquely their own.

In Indonesia, children learn the music of the gamelan orchestra by attending the puppet theater. From about the age of five, they progress through all the instruments, playing the most difficult ones when they are adult. The most important thing in the gamelan orchestra is for every player to contribute to the overall sound.

Make beaters for your drums

All kinds of things can be used as beaters for drums or xylophones. A knitting needle is ready to use, and a dowel can be shaped into a drumstick. Make a head for a bamboo cane from a wooden bead, a metal nut, a cork, or string. Wrap masking tape around the end of a stick if you want to make a soft sound. Use brush bristles to make a rustling noise.

A bow for strings

Traditionally, the best material for a bow is horse hair that has been rubbed with resin. However, horse hair is not easy to find today. A good alternative can be nylon thread, a guitar string, or stretched elastic.

Tie one end of the thread to the end of a thin garden cane. Bend the cane into a gentle arc, and tie the loose end of thread to the other end.

When you have made some of the instruments in this book, you might like to gather some friends together to help you make music. You could even form a band or an orchestra to entertain others.

In many cultures, music is based on the natural rhythms of speech. You can use this idea to build up a piece of music that involves as many instruments as you have available.

Begin with some words that you like, such as, "Can you hear the music of the spheres?" Say this sentence over and over again, listening to its rhythm.

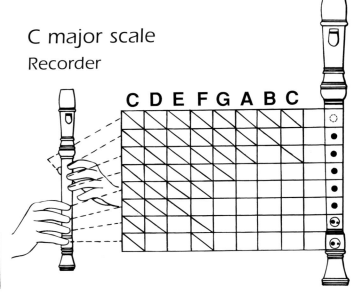

Start with a steady beat from sticks, a large drum, or a spike fiddle. Add instruments such as panpipes, guitar, and gender. Percussion instruments such as shaker, drum, and tambourine contribute their own rhythms. The prayer drum adds a burst of beats.

Tuning your instruments

If you know where to find the notes of the G major and C major scales on a piano or recorder, it will help you to tune the instruments you make.

C major scale
Recorder

G major scale
Piano

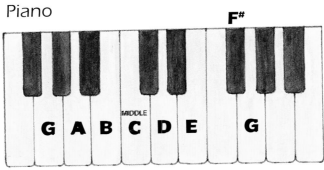

Glossary

aerophone: a musical instrument that works by vibrating air against a sharp edge

amplify: to make louder

bridge: a piece of wood or other material over which strings are stretched

calabash: the hard shell of a gourd or other tropical fruit that is used as a container

ceramic: made of pottery

chamois leather: soft leather from a sheep, goat, or deer

chordophone: a musical instrument that works by vibrating strings

conical: cone shaped

Coptic: belonging to the Copts, a group of Christians originally from Egypt

cylindrical: in the shape of a cylinder or tube

fingerboard: the part of a stringed instrument on which the player presses his or her fingers to change the pitch

flat: a musical term that means below the normal pitch of a note

gamelan orchestra: a group of Indonesian musicians who play at religious ceremonies, dances, and puppet plays

hide: skin of an animal

ideophone: a musical instrument that is designed to use the natural sounds of different materials

inlaid work: a way of decorating a wooden surface by fitting different colored woods into it

kiln: an oven used to dry clay

linguaphone: a musical instrument that works by vibrating a "tongue" of metal or other material

membranophone: a musical instrument that works by vibrating a skin, or membrane

modification: a change

morris dancer: traditional English folk dancer

Pan: the Greek god of woods and pastures

percussion: the act of tapping or striking a musical instrument

pitch: the quality of a musical note. Pitch is measured by the rate of vibrations.

pith: spongy tissue found in the stems of plants

pliable: flexible enough to bend without breaking

resonator: a box or container that makes a note sound louder

score: to mark with lines or scratches

sharp: a musical term that means higher than the normal pitch of a note

uncured: describes an animal skin before it has been treated to make it supple

vessel: a container such as a pot or jar

vibrate: to move back and forth very quickly

More Books to Read

Eyewitness: Music Neil Ardley (DK Publishing)

Let's Make Music!: Multicultural Songs and Activities Jessica Barron Turner and Ronny Susan Schiff (Hal Leonard)

Music and Dance (Discovering World Cultures) Neil Morris (Crabtree)

Rubber-Band Banjos and a Java Jive Bass: Projects and Activities on the Science of Music and Sound Alex Sabbeth (John Wiley)

Sound & Music Jon Richards (Copper Beech Books)

Story of the Orchestra Robert T. Levine (Black Dog & Leventhal)

Web Sites

Guide to Medieval and Renaissance Instruments
www.s-hamilton.k12.ia.us/antiqua/instrumt.html

Hawaiian Rhythm Instruments
www.ifccsa.org/hawainst.html

Instrument Encyclopedia
www.si.umich.edu/chico/instrument/

New York Philharmonic Kidzone
www.nyphilkids.org/main.phtml?

Index